Animal Habitats

The Chicken on the Farm

Text by Jennifer Coldrey

Photographs by Oxford Scientific Films

Gareth Stevens Publishing
Milwaukee

Where chickens live

Chickens are *domestic* birds. They are found mainly on farms where they are taken care of by people, in return for their eggs and meat. In olden days, the farmer would keep a small flock of chickens, enough to provide food for the family, with perhaps a few extra eggs to sell to local people. The chickens were free to roam around the farmyard, picking up food wherever they could.

On small farms today, chickens are still kept in this way. They are allowed outside during the day, when they can scratch around in the farmyard or wander freely in the fields. At night they are usually kept locked up in some sort of chicken coop where they are protected from foxes and other nighttime *predators*. The coop also provides shelter from the cold and wet and is a welcome place during the day, too. In it there are nest boxes where the hens can lay their eggs. On some farms, the chickens find shelter in barns and other buildings where there may also be warm, dry places to nest.

The chickens on this farm can wander freely in a grassy field during the daytime. They sleep in the chicken coop at night.

There are lots of places to explore in the farmyard, and chickens are not frightened of jumping onto walls.

Chickens allowed to live outside in this way are called "free-range." They get plenty of fresh air and sunshine during the day, as well as shelter when they need it. They are given grain and other food by the farmer, but they are also free to search for food of their own, such as grass, worms, and insects.

A farm is an unnatural *habitat* where the chickens are raised by humans. They are not free or wild birds. Yet free-range chickens live a fairly natural kind of life, even though their habitat is unnatural. Things are very different on big, modern chicken farms, where thousands of birds are crowded together in large, factory-like sheds. Sometimes the chickens are kept in small wire cages inside these sheds. They are fed on specially prepared food and spend their entire lives inside, under artificial light, without ever seeing the light of day. These chickens live in a very unnatural habitat.

A Red Jungle Fowl rooster crows proudly from his perch. All domesticated chickens are descended from this breed.

Different kinds of chicken

There are many different kinds of chicken in the world today, but they are all descended from the same ancestor, the wild Red Jungle Fowl of India and Southeast Asia. Wild jungle fowl still exist today in the forests of Southeast Asia. They were first tamed over 4,000 years ago by the local people. Later they spread or were introduced to other parts of the world, and people began to breed and rear them. Only the birds that were especially useful or beautiful were chosen for domestication and breeding. Over time, many different types of chicken were developed. Today there are well over a hundred different breeds and many more varieties.

Some breeds of chicken are large and heavy. They produce a lot of meat and are good for eating, but they do not lay many eggs. They include breeds like the Dorking, Old English, and Indian Game Fowl, most of which lay brown eggs. Other breeds are small and light, not much for eating, but extremely good at laying eggs. They include the White Leghorn, Minorca, and Ancona breeds, all of which lay white eggs. In between these two extremes are the all-purpose breeds, which are good both for eating and for laying eggs. They lay brown eggs and are often kept by farmers on smaller farms, since the hens are still good to eat when their egg-laying days are over. Some well-known all-purpose breeds are the Plymouth Rock, Rhode Island Red, Orpington, and Maran.

Some of the most popular farm chickens today are *hybrid* birds, produced by mating or crossing different breeds. This combines the good qualities of each breed. The White Leghorn hen crossed with a Rhode Island Red rooster is a favorite hybrid among poultry farmers. The hen is an outstanding egg-layer, sometimes producing as many as 300 eggs a year.

There are many other varieties of chicken, including some rather strange and fancy ones which people often keep as show birds. Some are covered in soft fluffy feathers or have feathery legs; others have bald necks or big feathery crests on top of their heads. Some breeds of chicken are very small. These are called *bantams*. They lay smaller and fewer eggs than the larger breeds, but they are often kept on small farms, because they are quite easy to keep and fun to watch. They also often make very good mothers.

The White Leghorn is one of the best egg-laying breeds of chicken. It lays as many as 300 white eggs in a year.

The Rhode Island Red is a popular breed on many farms. It lays brown eggs and is a good meat bird, too.

This magnificent rooster is larger and much more colorful than his hens. You can just see the spur on his right leg.

The chicken's body

Chickens come in various colors, shapes, and sizes, but they all have the same basic design. Their plump bodies are covered in soft, silky feathers, the neck or hackle feathers being especially glossy. The chicken's breast is keel-shaped, like a boat, and the tail sticks up at an angle to the body. Male chickens, called roosters, have long, arching tail feathers which sometimes droop down and touch the ground.

The colors vary according to the breed. Some chickens are mainly white, others black or brown, while many breeds have feathers which are speckled or striped with different colors, including gold, silver, black, red, blue, and green.

Most chickens have a rather small head with a strong, sharp beak. On each side of the head, around the eyes, are bare patches of skin, while beneath each ear a tuft of feathers or a fleshy lobe of skin often grows. Two flaps of loose skin, called *wattles*, hang down from the throat. On top of the head is a notched pink, fleshy crest call the *comb*. In some breeds the comb may be flat and knobbly; in others it is divided into two horns which fan out like a butterfly's wings. As with many birds, the males or roosters are more showy and colorful than the females or hens. The neck, back, and tail feathers of a rooster often glow with brilliant colors, and the comb and wattles are generally much larger than in the hen.

A rooster's head, showing the large pink comb and wattles. Notice the tuft of short pale feathers sticking out from his ear lobe.

Two strong legs support a chicken's body. The legs are covered with scales, and some breeds also have long, silky feathers growing right down to their toes. The large, strong feet are useful for walking and gripping. Chickens usually have four toes, although some breeds have five. Each toe ends in a sharp claw. Roosters have an extra spike or spur sticking out from the back of each leg. They use these spurs for fighting with each other. Chickens are stout, dumpy birds. They are better designed for walking than flying and cannot fly very far. Their wings are short and not very powerful, although they can flutter about and fly up onto a perch.

Chickens *molt* their feathers once a year, usually in the late summer. It takes anything from six to twelve weeks for the old feathers to be completely replaced by a new set. If you see a chicken with bare patches of skin, it probably means that it is molting.

Some breeds of chicken have soft, silky feathers growing right down their legs.

Free-range chickens find plenty to eat as they scratch on the ground and peck in the grass.

Food and feeding

Chickens that are free to roam around the farmyard will eat all kinds of natural food, including worms, grubs, insects, seeds, and young green shoots. Their sharp beaks are useful for pecking at seeds and for tearing at grass and other juicy plants. They use their feet and claws for scratching in the ground to help them find food. Chickens can be useful to the farmer, because they help clear away weeds and eat insect pests. In the past, a farmer would often put them out into the fields after the harvest, where the chickens cleaned up the ground before it was plowed ready for new crops.

Although free-range chickens can find their own food, the farmer usually feeds them, too. He or she gives them grain, either wheat or corn, and perhaps some specially prepared chicken feed bought from a supplier. This is made from ground grain and fish-meal, with extra minerals and vitamins added. It comes in the form of crumbs or pellets, or as a dry powdery bran or mash. The chickens are also fed scraps from the farmhouse — bits of potato, bacon rind, stale bread, or vegetables, all of which are a useful extra supply of food. Grass, fresh green vegetables, and other plant foods are especially valuable in the chicken's diet, because they contain important vitamins and minerals which are needed to keep the body healthy. Green foods also contain *pigments* which give the egg yolks a rich yellow color.

Chickens have to eat a certain amount of lime or calcium in order to make a good, strong shell around their eggs. Farmers sometimes feed them ground oyster shell or crushed limestone to make sure they are getting enough calcium.

Chickens have no teeth. They swallow their food whole and it passes into the crop, a bag-like pouch which stores and softens the food. The rough, hard bits are later ground up inside the gizzard, which is a second, bag-like stomach with thick muscular walls. Chickens need to take in small pieces of grit or stone which are churned around inside the gizzard, where they help to grind down food such as seeds and grain. Free-range chickens pick up bits of stone or gravel naturally, but birds kept permanently inside a coop have to be given grit to help them digest their food.

Chickens also need plenty of fresh water to drink.

Two chickens enjoy dust-bathing in the dry, dusty soil.

Habits and behavior

Modern chickens are highly domesticated birds, but they still show many of the same habits as their wild relatives. Wild jungle fowl live in noisy flocks in the forests where they *roost* in the trees and peck and scratch on the ground for food. Modern farmyard chickens also peck and scratch at the ground to find food.

When not busy feeding and excercising, chickens like to rest by perching above the ground on some sort of branch or pole. The farmer usually puts special perches in the coop, where the chickens can sleep or roost at night. In their ancient jungle home, perching up in trees and bushes kept the birds safe from enemies roaming the forest floor at night. When roosting, the toes of a chicken grip the perch tightly and the muscles lock into place, so that even if the bird goes to sleep, it doesn't fall off.

A chicken preens its feathers to keep them clean and free from parasites.

Like most birds, chickens try to keep their feathers in good condition. They clean them regularly by stroking or *preening* them with their beaks. They also like to dust-bathe in dry, dusty soil. To do this, a chicken either makes or finds a hollow in the ground. It then squats down and rubs its body in the earth, meanwhile fluffing out its feathers so that the fine, dry soil trickles over its body. Dust-bathing helps to get rid of fleas and other *parasites* on the skin and feathers. It also helps to keep the chickens cool in hot weather. Chickens sometimes trickle water over their feathers in hot weather too, but they normally hate getting wet and never bathe in water.

Chickens are sociable birds. They like to live in flocks, although they are often very quarrelsome and aggressive toward each other. Some birds are much stronger and more aggressive than others. They dominate the weaker ones. In any flock there is a definite social order, ranging from the weakest, most timid member to the strongest and most bossy bird. This is called the "pecking order." The weakest birds often get pecked and sometimes viciously attacked by stronger birds, especially if there is competition for food or for good places to sleep or nest.

Chickens are noisy birds, constantly squawking and clucking to each other. The roosters have the loudest calls, as anyone living in the country is bound to discover when awakened by their crowing at dawn.

Fights and squabbles are common among chickens, as the stronger
birds keep the weaker birds in their place.

Two roosters fighting on a farm in Costa Rica.

Courtship and mating

On small farms, the farmer often has a *cockerel,* or young rooster, living with the hens. The rooster is usually a proud, handsome creature, who likes to crow loudly and strut around the farmyard, showing off his fine plumage to the hens. It is never wise to keep more than one rooster with a small flock of hens, because two roosters are likely to become jealous rivals and fight vigorously with each other over the hens. Cockerels fight with their feet and claws, using the sharp spurs on their legs to kick and tear each other to pieces.

When mating, the rooster climbs on top of the hen.

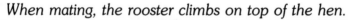

Chickens mate throughout the year, though not so much during the winter. A rooster will mate every two or three days. He mates with lots of different hens. When courting, a cockerel will preen his feathers and prance about near the hens. He often fluffs out his neck feathers to make a sort of ruff, and sometimes he raises one wing in his courtship display. When a hen is ready to mate, she squats down on the ground and the rooster climbs onto her from behind. He spreads his wings apart slightly to help balance on her back. As their tails come together, the rooster passes his *sperm* into the hen's body. The sperm swim up the hen's *oviduct* to fertilize her eggs.

It is only eggs that have been fertilized by a rooster that will eventually grow into chicks.

A rooster rests quietly with his hens in the farmyard.

This White Leghorn has just laid an egg. After she has laid an egg, a hen usually clucks loudly, as though proudly announcing its arrival.

Laying eggs

Hens lay eggs for most of their lives, whether or not the eggs have been fertilized by a rooster. They usually lay only one egg a day.

In the natural state, a wild hen would lay a *clutch* of fertile eggs and then she would stop to sit on her eggs until they hatched. On modern farms, however, the eggs are not usually fertile and they are taken away as soon as they are laid, to encourage the hens to go on laying. Domesticated hens have also been specially bred to continue laying and to produce much larger clutches than in the wild. The best egg-laying hens of today produce between 250 and 300 eggs a year, compared to the 25 to 50 eggs of the wild jungle fowl.

Hens like to have some sort of nest in which to lay their eggs. In the wild, they use a hollow on the ground, but on a farm, they are usually given special nesting boxes. Nesting boxes are made of wood and lined with hay or straw. It is best if they are kept about 12-18 inches (30-40 cm) up off the ground, so that other hens don't walk over the eggs or perhaps eat them. Hens prefer to nest in dark, warm places. Sometimes they find unusual corners of their own in the farmyard.

Inside the chicken coop there are rows of nesting boxes where the hens can lay their eggs.

It takes about a day for an egg to grow inside the hen's body. The tiny egg cells, with their yolk, are first produced in the hen's *ovary*. Each day one egg cell is released. It passes down the oviduct, where the layers of white are added around the yolk. A double skin or membrane is then laid down around the white, and finally the shell is added. The oval egg eventually comes out of the hen as she squats over the nest. Some hens lay white eggs and some lay brown. There is even one breed that lays blue- or green-shelled eggs.

When an egg is first laid, the shell is slightly moist, but it quickly dries and sets to form an outer skin. Free-range hens lay most eggs in the early part of the year when the days become longer. They lay fewer eggs in autumn, as the days shorten, and they may stop laying altogether during the winter. Hens on a modern poultry farm, under artificial light and heating, lay eggs continually all year round.

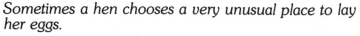

Sometimes a hen chooses a very unusual place to lay her eggs.

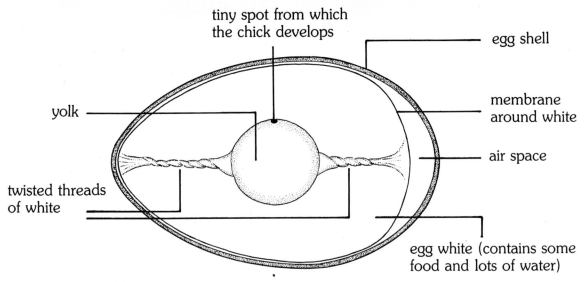

tiny spot from which
the chick develops

egg shell

yolk

membrane
around white

air space

twisted threads
of white

egg white (contains some
food and lots of water)

What a fresly laid egg looks like inside.

Growth inside the egg

A chicken's egg is full of goodness. It provides all the nourishment a growing chick will need and is very nutritious for humans, too. The yolk is especially rich in food, and the white provides a small amount of food as well as lots of water. Between the white and the shell, at the broad end of the egg, is an air space which will later be used by the young chick for breathing. The shell protects the *embryo* as it grows and prevents dirt and germs from getting inside the egg. Hundreds of tiny holes in the shell allow air to pass in and out so that the embryo can breathe.

When a fertilized egg is first laid, the baby chick is nothing more than a tiny white disc, 1/25 inch (1 mm) across, on top of the yolk. This slowly grows and develops into a baby chick. It is not long before the head, body and tail begin to take shape and, in three days, the embryo has a well-developed heart and blood supply. Gradually a network of blood vessels spreads across the yolk

A broody hen will sit on a clutch of eggs for three weeks, until they hatch.

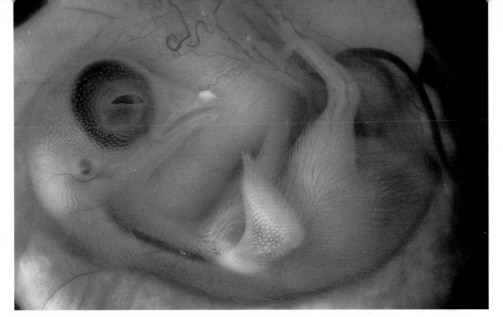

At only ten days old, this chick is about 1½ inches (40 mm) long and has a well-formed head and limbs. At this stage, the feathers are just starting to grow.

and white. The blood is used to carry food and water — and also oxygen from the air space — to the growing chick. Slowly the legs and wings begin to form, until by ten days old, the toes are showing and the feathers are starting to push through the skin. The baby chick continues to grow, feeding on the yolk and white, until it almost uses them up and finally fills the entire shell. It is ready to hatch in 21 days.

Young chicks will only grow from fertile eggs that are kept warm or *incubated.* The natural way to incubate eggs is for a *broody* hen to sit on them. But not all hens become broody, and fertile eggs from a non-broody hen sometimes have to be placed under a broody hen which is not the real mother. A broody hen is usually kept in a special coop or nesting box away from the noise and bustle of the other hens. Her nest should be warm and free from drafts, but it should also be damp. Otherwise the eggs will dry out and die. A nest on the ground is best, so that the moisture can seep up from below.

A broody hen usually clucks away contentedly while she sits on her nest. She ruffles up her feathers and presses her body against the eggs to keep them warm. Two or three times a day she will turn the eggs to warm them evenly. Most hens can brood about eight or nine eggs at a time, although a bantam can only manage five or six. A good broody hen will sit tight until the eggs hatch out. Some make such dedicated mothers that they have to be lifted off the nest for a short while each day to feed and get some exercise.

Broody hens are not used on big modern farms. Instead, the fertile eggs are placed in special heated cupboards called incubators. Here the eggs are turned mechanically and the temperature and moisture are kept just right for the development of the chicks.

A baby chick is wet and limp when it first hatches from the egg.

Hatching into young chicks

A few days before the eggs are ready to hatch, the chicks can be heard cheeping inside their shells and the hen clucks in reply. Then a tapping noise is heard as the first chick tries to break its way out of the egg. The baby bird chips away at the shell, using a special sharp nail on the end of its beak, called the "egg-tooth." It makes a rough line round the middle of the egg and finally breaks out by pushing the two halves of the shell apart. It can take up to 14 hours for a chick to hatch. The eggs in one clutch usually hatch within a few hours of each other, even though some will have been laid several days apart. This is because the chicks only start to develop when the whole clutch is laid and the hen begins to incubate the eggs.

The chick is wet and limp when it first hatches, but it soon dries out to become a fluffy ball of down. The egg-tooth drops off during the first day. Baby chicks are able to stand almost right away, and they will follow the hen as soon as she moves. For the first day or two they live on the remains of the yolk inside their bodies, but then they start to find food for themselves. As they run around after their mother, the hen teaches them to peck for the right food.

An hour or two after hatching, the chick's down has dried to form a fluffy, yellow coat.

The chicks keep warm, especially at night, by clustering under the wings and body of the hen. Their continual cheeping keeps them together and helps the mother to keep in touch with them. The farmer sometimes puts the family into a special coop with bars across the front. This is kept inside a small open pen. The hen stays inside the coop and cannot escape or desert the chicks. The chicks, meanwhile, can wander around freely inside the pen, able to scurry back between the bars to seek warmth and shelter under their mother.

On farms where there is no broody hen, the young chicks are reared inside, in special brooding pens or sheds. They are kept warm under electric lamps or heaters.

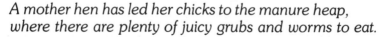

*A mother hen has led her chicks to the manure heap,
where there are plenty of juicy grubs and worms to eat.*

These young chickens, now ten weeks old, are living together in a poultry house where they have learned to perch.

Growing up

At two to three weeks old, the chicks start to lose their down and grow their first real feathers. Up to this stage it is very difficult to tell males from females, but it becomes easier as they get older. The feathers grow in a slightly different way on males and females, and the comb on a young rooster, or cockerel, starts to grow at four or five weeks, much earlier than on a young hen.

Chicks reared under a broody hen usually stay with her for several weeks. During the day they may be allowed out into the farmyard, but at night they will be safely penned in together. As the chicks grow, they gradually become more independent, until they finally wander away from the hen to lead separate lives of their own. Chicks reared in a brooding pen are normally allowed outside when they are four to six weeks old. They are often kept in an outside enclosed run and brought inside at night. At six weeks, the chicks are well-grown, and at nine or ten weeks, most young birds are moved into some kind of poultry house where they are given perches.

Young female chickens are called *pullets*. They are kept by farmers mainly for egg-laying. They will start to lay when they are five months old, and their scrawny pink combs are just beginning to redden. Their first eggs are rather small, but they gradually get bigger. Pullets cannot lay fertile eggs until they are fully mature at one year old. Chickens lay most eggs in their first year. They lay fewer eggs in the second year and even fewer after that. On big poultry farms, laying hens are only kept for their first eighteen months, after which they are killed for eating or to provide meat for various food products.

Young cockerels are kept either for breeding or to provide meat for the table. On special farms where chickens are reared only for eating, the young birds (both male and female) are fattened up quickly and killed at about nine weeks old, when they are young and tender. Chickens on an old-fashioned kind of farm that are not being killed for the table can expect to live much longer than this — sometimes up to 12 years or so.

At just over five months old, these young pullets have started to lay eggs.

The fox is one of the chicken's main enemies.

Enemies and other dangers

Although chickens are looked after and protected by people, they still have several enemies to fear. The fox is one of the worst of these enemies. Foxes hunt mainly at night and are often tempted into the farmyard to sniff around for any chickens they can find. It is most important that the chickens are locked up securely at night, because, if a fox breaks into a chicken coop, it usually causes havoc and kills many birds.

Other wild animals that may attack chickens on the farm include birds of prey, badgers, mink, weasels, stoats, and rats, although many of these animals will only take young chicks. If the chickens are kept in an enclosure out in the open, the farmer must make sure the fencing goes down deep into the ground, otherwise foxes, badgers and rats will burrow underneath and into the run. Rats and mice are always a problem around the farm. They will eat chicken feed whenever they get the chance, and rats will steal eggs, as well as kill young chicks. Even some of the other farmyard animals can be a threat to chickens. Dogs often chase them and cats may pounce on young chicks and kill them.

Chickens have very few defenses against their enemies. They are nervous birds and panic very easily. Sometimes a rooster will try to defend the hens by fighting off an enemy, but his courage often fails and he soon gives up. Chickens have much smaller enemies, too. These include parasites, such as fleas, ticks, lice, and mites, which live on the chicken's skin and feathers. These parasites weaken the birds and cause a lot of irritation. They sometimes spread diseases and can cause death in young chicks. Sometimes chickens have to be sprayed with *insecticides* to get rid of the parasites on their bodies.

Chickens catch cold easily. They also suffer from other diseases which can spread very quickly through a chicken coop. The farmer can help to prevent these diseases by keeping the coop clean and disinfected and by making sure there is plenty of ventilation. Also, the chickens should be kept warm and dry when they are inside.

Rats can be a nuisance on the farm when they steal chicken feed. They also kill young chicks and eat eggs.

Cockfighting, from an 18th century Persian text now in the British Museum.

Chickens and humans

Chickens have been kept and reared by humans for centuries. As long ago as 1400 B.C. the Chinese were known to keep domestic hens; so did the ancient Egyptians, followed by the Greeks and Romans. As people traveled to different parts of the world, they took their animals with them. Chickens had been brought to Western Europe and Britain by 100 A.D., but they did not reach the Americas until the 16th century, where they were introduced by Spanish soldiers and explorers.

This fancy breed of rooster has a huge crest of feathers on top of his head.

Throughout the world, people have bred and reared chickens for various purposes. In Greece, Rome, and Persia, in ancient days, chickens were used for religious sacrifices, while the Chinese and other Asiatic people were mainly interested in cockfighting. Here the birds were bred for bravery and for the urge to fight and kill. Cockfighting was considered a great sport, and people would lay bets on the birds they hoped would win. Sometimes the roosters' spurs would be fitted with iron spikes to make the fight more bloody. Cockfighting later became popular in Europe and other parts of the world, and it was not until the middle of the 19th century that it was banned in many countries as a cruel and vicious sport.

Other people are more interested in chickens as show birds. These chickens are bred for their colorful plumage or for their extraordinary combs, crests, and wattles. They include certain game fowl and many of the bantams. One of the most spectacular show birds is the Long-tailed Yokohama chicken, a Japanese bird with a long, graceful tail up to 20 feet (6 m) long.

Chickens have always been used as food by humans, but it was only about a hundred years ago that people began to breed chickens seriously for their eggs and meat. Since then, poultry has become big business and many breeds of chickens have been produced especially for the market. Some birds are particularly good for laying eggs, while others make very good meat birds. The general-purpose birds can be used for laying eggs and for eating, while some breeds are kept mainly for crossbreeding, to produce new varieties of chicken.

It is not just farmers that raise chickens. Many people have them in their backyard or garden. Not only do they give us eggs and meat, but they are also interesting and fun, and they provide manure for the garden. Some live to a ripe old age and escape being eaten by becoming pets.

Silkie chickens have very soft, fluffy feathers. This is a Chinese Silkie bantam, often kept as a show bird.

Thousands of birds are crowded together in this broiler operation.

Life on a modern poultry farm

At one time, most chickens kept on farms were free-range birds, allowed outside during the day, but kept in a coop at night. These birds provided enough eggs and meat to feed the whole population. However, during the last forty years or so, the human population has grown rapidly, and there is a much bigger demand for eggs and meat. People living in towns and cities have no room to keep chickens, and, even in the country, there is not enough land to spare for keeping the numbers of chickens needed to feed everybody. So nowadays, most chickens are farmed on huge, modern poultry farms, where thousands of birds are reared or kept indoors. Some farms specialize in egg production and only keep laying hens. Others specialize in birds for eating, called *broilers*. There are also special farms for incubating and hatching eggs, while others rear young chicks until they are ready to lay eggs or to be used for breeding.

Chickens may be kept in several different ways on a large poultry farm. Sometimes they are kept in a broiler operation. This is a large, windowless shed, where the lights are left on for about 17 hours a day. The concrete floor is covered with a thick layer of wood shavings, straw, or peat, and food and water are supplied in special troughs. There are perches for the chickens to roost on and nest boxes along the sides where it is slightly darker. There are sometimes as many as 20,000 chickens in one shed, and the atmosphere gets very smelly and noisy. A lot of fighting and squabbling goes on in these crowded conditions, and the farmer sometimes has to trim off the tip of each bird's beak to stop it from pecking and pulling out the feathers of other birds. Mainly broiler chickens are kept in a broiler house.

Egg-laying hens may be kept on egg-laying farms, or layer operations. Here, the hens are kept in wire cages about 20 inches (50 cm) square, with often three to five hens in one cage. They are arranged inside sheds in long rows, several tiers high. The hens eat and drink from a trough in front of them. The wire-mesh floors of the cages are sloping, so the eggs roll down and into a collecting tray in front. The droppings fall through the cages and are cleaned away from below. As in the broiler house, the hens live in artifical light, which is kept on every day to encourage them to lay more eggs. Egg-laying hens are kept warm and clean. They are safe from enemies and the cold weather outside, and they have a constant supply of food and water. However, many people think it is a very cruel and unnatural way of keeping hens. The birds are so tightly crowded, they have no space to walk about and flap their wings, nor can they scratch or dust-bathe in the normal way. Their feet and legs often become deformed and weak because they do not get enough exercise, while the hens in any one cage are likely to peck and even kill each other unless their beaks are trimmed.

Free-range chickens take up more space and are more expensive to rear than chickens kept on modern poultry farms. However, many people would prefer chickens to be farmed in the free-range way. They think their eggs and meat taste much better and that it is worth paying more money to buy them.

Unlike chickens in many layer operations, the hens on this egg farm do get some fresh air and daylight during the summer months.

This woman is feeding the poultry on her farm. A White Silkie hen and her chicks share the food with various kinds of ducks and geese.

Friends and neighbors

Chickens on a modern poultry farm never see any other animals, except for the people who come in to feed them and collect the eggs. But on the more traditional kind of farm there are normally plenty of other animals around. The farmer may well keep other poultry, including ducks, geese, or turkeys. These birds seem to mix quite well with the chickens as they search for food during the day. At night, however, they are usually kept in separate huts.

Ducks and geese sometimes desert their eggs. They are not always as good mothers as hens, and so the farmer sometimes uses a broody hen to hatch and rear young ducklings and goslings. Duck and goose eggs take longer to hatch than chicken eggs, but a good broody hen will usually sit until the eggs hatch out. After hatching, the adopted youngsters will accept the hen as their own mother and will follow her everywhere.

Sometimes a broody hen is used to rear young ducklings or goslings in place of her own chicks. The youngsters have to be introduced very carefully, one by one, under the sitting hen, in exchange for her own chicks. The strangers must be the same size and color as her own chicks, or she will reject them. Sometimes a broody hen may be able to rear her own chicks as well as some adopted ones.

These chickens are not worried by the cat that has gotten into their run to look for food.

Other animals on the farm may include pigs, goats, horses, cows, and sheep. And there are bound to be some cats and dogs around, too. Cats do not generally bother hens too much, and they help keep down the mice and rats around the farm. Wild birds, including sparrows, starlings, and pigeons, come to the farm to feed on the spilled grain and any other food they can find. They rarely eat enough to cause any harm, but they sometimes bring in diseases which are picked up by the chickens.

On some free-range farms, chickens are allowed out in the fields during the day. There are often cows or sheep in the same field. The grazing of these large animals makes it easier for the chickens to find the young short grasses. By scratching on the ground, chickens help to spread manure over the field, and this helps the farmer.

Chickens and cows sometimes live together in the same field.

Life on the farm

On a free-range type of farm, the chickens depend for their food on the grass and insects which they find outside, as well as on the grain the farmer gives them. Their diet is a mixture of plants and small animals. Whatever they eat is used to build up and strengthen their bodies, while much of what a hen eats also goes to form the goodness inside its eggs. All this food is eventually passed on to the predators that eat the chickens, so forming a food chain.

Human beings are the main consumers of chickens. So, it is especially interesting for us to know what they are eating, since this will eventually end up inside us. On modern farms, the special feeds that chickens are given are still made largely from natural plants and animals. They include ground-up grains and fish, as well as other plant and animal extracts. This diagram shows some of the food chains linking what chickens eat to our own diet.

Food chain

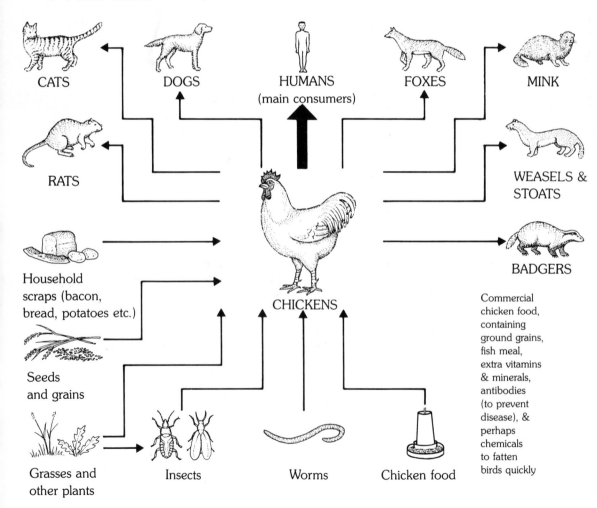

CATS

DOGS

HUMANS
(main consumers)

FOXES

MINK

RATS

WEASELS &
STOATS

Household
scraps (bacon,
bread, potatoes etc.)

BADGERS

CHICKENS

Seeds
and grains

Commercial
chicken food,
containing
ground grains,
fish meal,
extra vitamins
& minerals,
antibodies
(to prevent
disease), &
perhaps
chemicals
to fatten
birds quickly

Grasses and
other plants

Insects

Worms

Chicken food

These chickens look healthy and contented as they scratch among the nettles on a free-range farm.

Chickens living on a small, old-fashioned type of farm usually have a pleasant, healthy life. They are given both food and shelter by the farmer, but they are also free to scratch around in the open and to look for natural foods of their own.

Life may not seem so good on a modern poultry farm, where the chickens are kept inside in very crowded conditions. They never get out into the fresh air and sunshine, and they are fed on artificial foods. However, they are always kept warm and well-fed, and they never have any outside enemies to fear.

In whatever way they are kept, most chickens end up being killed and eaten. During their short lives, it is important that we look after them well. Although they are no longer wild birds, we can at least make sure that their habitat on the farm is as natural as possible. Most people would agree that free-range chickens undoubtedly have the freest and most natural kind of life.

Glossary

These new words about chickens appear in the text in *italics,* just as they appear here.

bantam........a miniature breed of chicken

broiler........a chicken reared for its meat

broody........the maternal instinct of a hen, making it want to sit on eggs and rear chicks

clutch.........a set of eggs

cockerel.......a male chicken under one year old

comb.........the fleshy part on top of a chicken's head

domestic.......tamed and kept by humans

embryo........the very early stages of an animal's development, before it is born or hatched

habitat........the place where an animal or plant lives

hybrid.........an animal or plant produced by crossing or mating two different breeds or varieties

incubated......(of eggs) kept warm so that they will hatch

insecticides.....chemicals used to kill insect pests

molt..........to shed feathers and replace them with new ones

ovary.........a female sex organ which produces eggs

oviduct........the long, winding tube leading from the hen's ovary to the opening under her tail

parasites.......animals (or plants) which live and feed on others

pigments......colored substances found in animals and plants

predators......animals that kill and eat other animals

preening.......cleaning the feathers by stroking and combing them with the bill

pullet.........a female chicken under one year old

roost..........to sleep or rest

sperm.........(short for spermatozoa) male sex cells

wattles........loose flaps of skin hanging down from either side of a chicken's face

Reading Level Analysis: SPACHE 2.9, FRY 2-3, FLESCH 95 (very easy), RAYGOR 3, FOG 4, SMOG 3

Library of Congress Cataloging-in-Publication Data

Coldrey, Jennifer. The chicken on the farm.

(Animal habitats)

Summary: Text and photographs depict chickens feeding, breeding, and defending themselves in their natural habitats.

1. Chickens — Juvenile literature. [1. Chickens] I. Oxford Scientific Films. II. Title. III. Series.

SF487.5.C648   1986   636.5   86-5716

ISBN 1-55532-092-9

ISBN 1-55532-067-8 (lib. bdg.)

North American edition first published in 1987 by

Gareth Stevens, Inc.
7221 West Green Tree Road   Milwaukee, WI 53223, USA.

Conceived, designed, and produced by Belitha Press Ltd., London.

Typeset by Ries Graphics ltd., Milwaukee.
Printed in Hong Kong by South China Printing Co.
Series Editor: Jennifer Coldrey.
U.S. Editors: MaryLee Knowlton & Mark J. Sachner.
Art Director: Treld Bicknell.   Design: Naomi Games.
Line Drawings: Lorna Turpin.
Scientific Consultants: Gwynne Vevers and David Saintsing.

Photography: **Oxford Scientific Films Ltd.** for pp. 1, 2, 3, 5 *both,* 7 *above,* 8, 9, 10 *both,* 11, 12 *below,* 13, 14, 15 *both,* 16, 20, 29 *below,* and 31 (photographer G.I. Bernard): p. 4 (photographer David Cayless); pp. 6, 12 *above,* and 19 *above* (photographer David Thompson); p. 7 *below,* 24 *below,* and 25 (photographers P. and W. Ward); pp. 17, 23 (photographer Peter Parks); p. 18 (photographer J. A. L. Cooke); p. 19 *below* (photographer Tony Allen); pp. 21, 26, 28, 29 *above,* and back cover (photographer Avril Ramage); p. 22 (photographer Robin Redfern); p. 27 (photographer Z. Leszczynsky); p. 24 *above* (courtesy of the British Museum); **Bruce Coleman ltd.** for the front cover.